Bibliographic information published by the German National Library:

The German National Library lists this publication in the National Bibliography; detailed bibliographic data are available on the Internet at http://dnb.dnb.de .

Imprint:

Copyright © 2017 GRIN Verlag, Open Publishing GmbH
Print and binding: Books on Demand GmbH, Norderstedt Germany
ISBN: 9783668456471

This book at GRIN:

http://www.grin.com/en/e-book/366937/the-analysis-of-financial-statements

Mike G.

The Analysis of Financial Statements

Optimize your trading strategy!

GRIN Publishing

GRIN - Your knowledge has value

Since its foundation in 1998, GRIN has specialized in publishing academic texts by students, college teachers and other academics as e-book and printed book. The website www.grin.com is an ideal platform for presenting term papers, final papers, scientific essays, dissertations and specialist books.

Visit us on the internet:

http://www.grin.com/

http://www.facebook.com/grincom

http://www.twitter.com/grin_com

Financial Statements Analysis

A quick look at the actual and previous balance sheets of the Swedish clothing retailer H&M raises the question how they managed to keep their liabilities that low. This is mainly due to the excessive usage of (operating) lease agreements which aren't shown in the balance sheet as liability; only the rent expense is included in the statement of profit & loss. Many investors, therefore, deem H&M to be a very stable and profitable enterprise. Such misbeliefs can lead to high losses of the investors or even to a global financial crisis as seen 2007/08. Large (global) companies are trained to stretch federal law for their own benefit. With financial statement analysis, such tricks of the firms can be identified and the company's intrinsic value will be revealed. For sure, it is hard work to do and it is furthermore very time-consuming, but it is worth the pain when your investments pay off. This text will introduce the most important adjustments you can undertake to correct the financial statements from so-called "window-dressing".

Content

General information.

- Perspective of an equity investor now.
- Sometimes accounting methods are over-cautious to prevent under-estimations.
- Value reflects the expected future cash flows (max. price * volume; min. costs * investment).
- Financial statements analysis uncover value drivers.

Apple Case Study.

- $gross\ margin = \dfrac{gross\ profit}{total\ sales}$ Measure of profitability.
- Apple's gross margin decreased, but is expected to increase to 38%.
  - Expectations made by analysts (information intermediates).
  - Extrapolation of future, going concern assumption.
- Numbers announced disappointed expectations (1% lower) and share price decreases (-5.1%).
- Announced with the actual numbers, Apple's expectations for the next period are announced too.
- Reduction in gross profit should be related to changed accounting method, deferred revenue increased.
  - Over 900m of revenue is deferred over the next 8 quarters.

Deferred Revenue by Apple.

- Selling price of an Apple product doesn't reflect profit, it includes cash for future software upgrades (which are free for product users) → Liability arises.
- Those future software upgrades are still outstanding and will realize revenue over the next 8 quarters.

Deferred Revenue Liability 20	Revenue 1Q after sale 2.5 Revenue 2Qs after sale 2.5 Revenue 3Qs after sale 2.5 Revenue 4Qs after sale 2.5 Revenue 5Qs after sale 2.5 Revenue 6Qs after sale 2.5 Revenue 7Qs after sale 2.5 Revenue 8Qs after sale 2.5	vs.	Operating Expenses from creating software upgrades of unknown size over eight (+/-?) quarters

- Related to the matching concept (cost and revenue should match the same time they occur).

- Realize revenue only when it occurs.
- Apple offers more software services with free upgrades for customers, therefore the deferred revenue per iPhone 5 increased from $ 5-25 to $ 20-40.
- **Adjust the gross margin for the effect of increased deferrals.**

	Revenue Forecast		
	Low	High	Mid
Revenue (bn)	55.00	58.00	56.50
Gross Margin (High)	37.5%	37.5%	37.5%
Implied COGS (bn)	34.375	36.25	35.313
	Revenue Forecast		
	Low	High	Mid
Revenue	55.90	58.90	57.40
COGS	34.375	36.25	35.313
Adjusted Gross Margin	38.5%	38.5%	38.5%

- Revenue (= profit = total sales) as well as the gross margin are given.
- 1) Calculate the total revenue (sales – (sales * gross margin))
- 2) Add the announced amount of deferrals (900m) to the revenue and re-calculate the gross margin.
  => Regarding those information the market price re-stabled.
- **Conclusions of this situation.**
- Apple could have announced this change in accounting methods, but in this situation the share price volatility increased and also the risk → not demanded by shareholders.
- By deferring, they create a buffer against future decreasing revenue because they receive revenue by this deferrals for sure.
- Market price reacts to deviations from expectations about future value drivers.
  → Even a "small" deviation can move equity value a lot.
- Fundamental analysis pays off: Can uncover "insider information".
- Transparency can pay off: Announcing changes can prevent for volatility.

Managing Expectations.

- Suppose a total of 40 analysts work on Apple and try to estimate its future EPS.
- The mid of all those 40 estimations reveals the "consensus estimation".

$$EPS = \frac{earnings}{shares\ outstanding} \qquad consensus\ estimate = \frac{\Sigma\ 40\ forecasts}{40}$$

- Most companies meet or beat the consensus.
  - Statistics would expect a normal distribution related to the bell curve.
  - Accounting cosmetics and "cooking the books" make the company meet its expectations

because managements bonuses are related to meeting or beating the expectations.

Performance vs. consensus estimates.

- Distinguish three groups of companies.
  - Consistently beating (a.l. 4 out of 7 years) the consensus estimations.
  - Inconsistent beating (less than 4 beatings out of 7 years).
  - Consistently missing (a.l. 4 out of 7 years) the consensus estimations.
- Companies from group 1 & 2 with high growth and/or high ROIC have positive returns to shareholders.
- Only low growth and ROIC or companies from group 3 generate negative TRS.
  => Meeting expectations isn't the only criteria determining the value of a company.

Company Valuation (equity perspective).

~ company is only equity-financed, firm value = equity value ~
- Company must generate economic profit // economic rents // excess returns.
  - Invest in projects with positive NPV (= investment return is higher than cost of capital).
  - Cost of debt: interest rate as compensation for lenders for taking the risk of borrowing.
  - Cost of equity: investors face opportunity costs, therefore company must offer at least some "interest rate" to make investors not regret their investment. Theoretical interest expense is not related to cash flows (can be by dividends) or changes in the financial statements.
    → If paying dividends, they must at least equal this theoretical interest rate of equity.
- Profitable growth is a result of competitive advantages like patents or economies of scale.

Dividend discount model.

- Evaluation of company's value by looking at it's dividends.
- Calculation of PV by using dividends as expected future cash flow.
- $PV = market\ value = \sum_{t=1}^{\infty} \dfrac{D_t}{(1+r)^t}$
- $PV_{perpetuity} = \dfrac{D}{r}$ if cash flow will occur constantly forever (perpetuity).
- PV equals the market value, but the question is how does this takes <u>profitability</u> and <u>growth</u>

into account.

- Calculation of **excess return**.

  - $Excess\ return = RoE - Cost\ of\ Equity\ Capital = ROE - r = \dfrac{Dividend}{Equity\ Investment} - r$

- With this we can calculate the **economic profit** per period.

  $Economic\ profit = Excess\ return * Equity\ Investment = \left(\dfrac{D}{EI} - r\right) * Equity\ Investment$

- "**Value added**" equals economic profit divided by equity cost.

  - $Value\ Added = \dfrac{\left(\dfrac{D}{Equity\ investment} - r\right) * Equity\ investment}{r} = \dfrac{economic\ profit}{equity\ cost}$

- Calculated market value of a company is a combination of equity investment and "value added".

  => **Key value drivers in this model are: RoE, economic profit, excess rate.**

Residual income model // economic profit valuation model.

- Because not every company pays out dividends, another valuation model became common.
- **Residual income** is amount of money exceeding total equity costs on book value.
- $RI_t = NI._t - r * CE_{t-1}$ Residual income = net income – equity costs * changes in equity.
- Consider the following $RI_t = NI._t - r * CE_{t-1} = (ROE_t - r) * CE_{t-1}$
- Given this information we can calculate the market value by looking at profitability and growth as the following.

  - $PV = CE + \sum\limits_{t=1}^{\infty} \dfrac{RI_t}{(1+r)^t} = CE + \dfrac{NI._t - r * CE_{t-1}}{(1+r)^t} = CE + \dfrac{(ROE_t - r) * CE_{t-1}}{(1+r)^t}$

  - CE = Equity investment = indicator of growth.
  - Following term indicated the profitability of the company.
  - In terms of perpetuity the term below the fraction line reduced to r.

  - $PV_{perpetuity} = CE + \sum\limits_{t=1}^{\infty} \dfrac{RI_t}{r}$

  => **Key value drivers in this model are: residual income, net income, RoE.**

- **Overview of both methods.**

  - Dividend discount model (normal): $PV = market\ value = \sum\limits_{t=1}^{\infty} \dfrac{D_t}{(1+r)^t}$

5

- Dividend discount model (perpetuity): $PV_{perpetuity} = \dfrac{D}{r}$

- Residual income model (normal): $PV = CE + \sum\limits_{t=1}^{\infty} \dfrac{RI_t}{(1+r)^t}$

- Residual income model (perpetuity): $PV = CE + \sum\limits_{t=1}^{\infty} \dfrac{RI_t}{r}$

Example company valuation.

- Company A has constant profits of $ 1 and pays out all of this as dividends. A has equity of $ 6 and required return on equity rate is 10% (theoretical interest rate, always given).
- **Dividends discount model.**
- Value of the company is 10, regarding the NPV calculation for perpetuity.
- $market\ value\ (regarding\ dividend\ discount\ model) = \dfrac{D}{r} = \dfrac{1}{0.1} = 10$
- Equity investment = 6 (regarding to the information given in the text above).
- $Value\ Added = \dfrac{\left(\frac{1}{6} - 0.1\right) * 6}{0.1} = 4$
- Market value (10) = Equity investment (6) + Value Added (4)
- **Residual income model.**
- $PV = CE + \sum\limits_{t=1}^{\infty} \dfrac{RI_t}{r} = 6 + \dfrac{1 - 0.1 * 6}{0.1} = 6 + 4 = 10$
- Because we know that 6 represents our equity investment, we directly see the value added and how the market value of 10 is split up.

- **Key value drivers.**
- Return on Equity: results from competitive advantage.
- Growth: primary "sales growth", only creates value if ROE is exceeding equity costs.

- **Basic steps underlying all valuation models.**
- (1) Forecast: Revenues & Margins (income statement), Investment (balance sheet).
- (2) Derive: Cash flows, dividends, economic profit (calculated by forecasts).
- (3) Discounting: Calculate the present value of the forecasted and calculated key numbers.

- **Valuation of non-dividend-paying companies.**
  - Company never paying out dividends is worthless.
    - You could buy the share with expectation to sell it for a higher price, but who wants to buy this share? Another one expecting the share price to raise, but at some point this chain ends.
  - Most companies decided to plow back profits for future investments, but this doesn't mean they are worthless. Our calculations are open to periods of time with dividends of zero, but sometimes there must be a dividend, otherwise the company is worthless.
  - Companies paying high dividends are valued higher (dividend discount model), but have less retained earnings, a smaller growth and will soon be less valuable.
  - Companies with small or no dividends grow (very) fast, but they need enough attractive investments to use the capital.

Valuation of a company with financial obligation (entity perspective).

- Now entity perspective, firm value = equity value and debt value.
- Important ratios are the following.
  - **Return on net operating assets** = net operating income / net operating assets

$$RNOA = \frac{NOI}{NOA}$$

  - **Return on Equity (RoE)** = NOI over Equity
  - **Cash Return on Debt** = Interest expense over NOI (equivalent for cash return on equity).
  - **Dividend payout ratio** = dividends over net income.
- Entity perspective focuses on revenue generated by operating activities independent to its financing.
  => Create a simplified balance sheet and income statement.
- **How to simplify the balance sheet.**
  - Invested Capital = all financing activities (equity + debt (exclude: payables)).
    → Therefore payables are also subtracted from total assets.
  - $Net\ Operating\ Assets\ (NOA) = Total\ Assets - Payables = Invested\ Capital$
  - $Operating\ Assets = Operating\ Liabilities + Debt + Equity$
  - With those simplifications the balance sheet will only consist of NOP and IC (and has to

7

balance!).

→ Very simple classification, more detailed later on.

- **How to simplify the income statement.**

  - $Operating\ Income = EBIT = operating\ sales - operating\ CoGS$

  - Net Operating Income (NOI) is equal to Net Operating Profit after Taxes (NOPAT).

  - $NOI = NOPAT = Net\ Income + (1 - tax\ rate)* \ 10 = EBIT - Tax$

  - Tax shield: Do not add the whole tax expense on net income (net income + tax $\neq$ NOI). Tax expense is tax deductible, reduces the taxable operating income, therefore more capital is left after taxation. Increasing debt reduces total amount of taxes paid and can enhance net income.

  - $Net\ Financing\ Expense\ (NFE) = Interest\ expense * (1 - interest\ rate)$

  - $Interest\ expense = NFE + Tax\ shield = NFE + (interest\ expense * interest\ rate)$

  - Furthermore the following is important.

  - $Net\ income = net\ operating\ income\ (NOI) - net\ financing\ expense\ (NFE)$.

- **How the simplified financial statements look like at the end.**

Balance sheet simplified (converted)			
Net Operating Assets	200	Invested Capital	200

Income Statement simplified (converted)		
Net Operating Income	80	Operating
Net Financing Expense	8	Financing
Net Income	72	

- **Interpretation from the entity perspective.**

  - Company received 200 and purchased 200 assets with expectation of future economic benefit.

  - Owned assets generated NOI of 80, which can (and has to) be distributed among investors.

  - Return on invested capital $ROIC = \dfrac{NOI}{IC}$ is important value driver.

  - Return on net operating assets $RNOA = \dfrac{NOI}{NOA}$ is an important ratio (the higher, the better).

  - WACC is the weighted average cost of capital, the mix of equity and debt cost.

  - $WACC = \dfrac{Equity}{total\ assets} * r_{equity} + \dfrac{Debt}{total\ assets} * d_{debt} * (1 - tax\ rate)$.

  => Only if ROIC or RNOA is greater than WACC than the company creates value.

Summary.

- Excess return captures the competitive advantage, reveals the company's primary value drivers.

- RoE depends on profitability, turnover and leverage.
- Equity perspective (NI) vs. entity perspective (NOI).
- ROIC = RNOA = assessing the operating activities of the company, not distorted by financing structure of the company.

- **Residual net operating income to all investors.**
  - $RNOI_t = NOI_t - WACC * NOA_{t-1} = (RNOA_t - WACC) * NOA_{t-1}$.
  - Therefore **company's value** equals
  - $P = NOA_0 + \sum_{t=1}^{\infty} \dfrac{NOI_t - WACC * NOA_{t-1}}{(1+w)^t}$.
  - And in case of **perpetuity**
  - $P = NOA_0 + \sum_{t=1}^{\infty} \dfrac{NOI_1 - WACC * NOA_0}{w}$.

- **Traditional DCF valuation.**
  - C = Cash flow to all investors $\quad C_t = NOI_t - (NOA_t - NOA_{t-1}) = D_t + I_t * (1 - tax) - \Delta debt_t$
    - Deduction of increases in retained earnings to make outcome more reliable.
  - $P = NOA_0 + \sum_{t=1}^{\infty} \dfrac{NOI_t - WACC * NOA_{t-1}}{(1+WACC)^t} = \sum_{t=1}^{\infty} \dfrac{C_t}{(1+WACC)^t}$.
  - DCF to all investors is equal to residual income to all investors.
  - Therefore residual income to equity investors equals DCF to equity investors D = net distribution to equity holders (dividends + stock repurchases – issued equity).
  - $D_t = NI._t - (CE_t - CE_{t-1})$.
  - $P_E = CE_0 + \sum_{t=1}^{\infty} \dfrac{NI._t - r * CE_{t-1}}{(1+r)^t} = \sum_{t=1}^{\infty} \dfrac{D_t}{(1+r)^t}$.
  - Companies want stable or increasing dividends, but net income is fluctuating, therefore by stock repurchases or raising of equity dividends can be influenced.
    - E.g. EPS, the denominator will decrease, earnings aren't decreasing, only cash.
  - **IPO vs. SEO.**
    - Initial public offering is only done in case of a private company is turned into a public one.
    - Seasoned equity offer means the issuance of additional shares to the market.

Concept of Economic Value Added (EVA) by Stewart.

- $EVA = (RNOA - WACC) * NOA = (ROIC - WACC) * IC$.
- Shows management how to increase shareholders value.
  - Increase of return generated by the investment; decrease total cost of capital; reallocate capital invested to projects with higher NPV.

- **Conclusions of entity perspective.**
  - In the entity perspective the firm's value consists of the value of equity and the value of debt.

$$P_E = CE_0 + \frac{NI_t - r * CE_{t-1}}{r} \qquad P_D = Debt_0 + \frac{I_t - d * Debt_{t-1}}{d}$$

Equity Value   Value Added   Debt Value   Value Added = 0

- In contrast to the equity value, debt doesn't grow additionally (only compound interest effect).
- Calculate company's equity value either by calculating the whole value and subtract the deb value or directly calculate the equity value with adjusted net income after interest.

- **Excess Return.**
  - $ROIC - WACC = Excess\ Return$ Should increase over the company's useful lifetime, but is observed to decrease after a few years.
  - Resulted in losing a competitive advantage, changing market conditions, etc.
  - In case of negative excess return (except in the start-up phase), the company will face bankruptcy or illiquidity.
  - **Operating Leverage.**
    - Naturally there are some industries requiring high variable costs (retailer, wholesaler) or high fixed costs (production).
    - Companies with high fixed costs are more sensitive towards changing sales (increase will increase profits proportionally higher because of economies of scale & v.v.).
      => High operating leverage normally tends to cause more volatile returns.
  - **Durability of high excess returns.**
    - High excess return in a market will attract new entrants and decrease the individual excess rates → In markets with pure competition therefore all excess rates are zero.

- Question is why to enter markets if expectation of making no profits at all.
  - Find a competitive advantage to ensure excess returns.
    => Nevertheless, in the long-rune we expect the excess return to be equal to WACC.
- **Mean-reversion of RoE.**
- High RoE raises competitors attention, prices are lowered and new competitors arise.
- Reaction of the first company will decrease its own profitability and lower it's RoE.
  - If companies are facing negative RoE, investors tend to quit and this "take-away" of equity will increase the RoE again.
- Mean-reversion tends to establish a constant range of 8-12%.
    => Pharmaceutical industry reports the highest RoE because R+D costs are expensed, therefore equity and assets are underestimated.

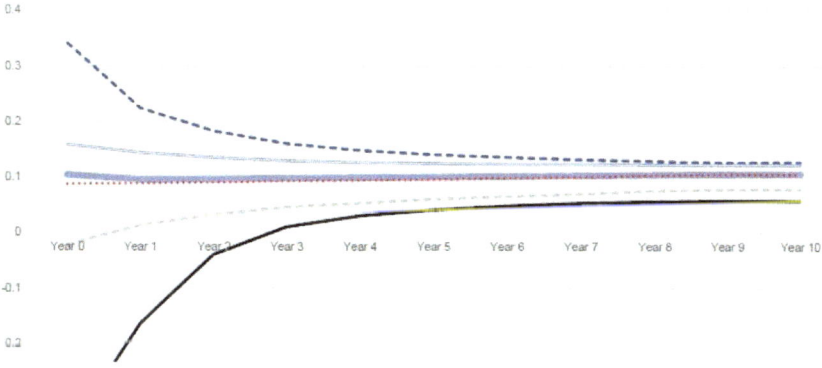

- This effect is also observed for (sales) growth.
  - Tend to mean-revert much quicker and establish a constant value of 8-9%.
- Market is limited, growth is only possible if stealing from competitiors, but they will try this too.
- Initially a strong growth rate is easier to achieve than later on because maintaining growth over the time against increasing competitors is a more difficult task.

Financing Leverage Effect.

- Regardless, If calculating company's value by entity or equity perspective won't change the result → Theorem or irrelevant capital structure by Modigliani & Miller.

- But we observe that the RoE is different (higher) if the company carries debt.

$$RoE = \frac{NI}{Sales} * \frac{Sales}{Total\ Assets} * \frac{Total\ Assets}{Equity} = \frac{NI}{Equity}$$

profit margin   turnover   leverage

- With increasing debt, the total leverage is increasing and influencing RoE.
- Looking at example numbers for a company with total assets of 6 and NOI of 1 in term of changing capital structure reveals the following results.

	0	1	2	3	4	5
Debt	0	1	2	3	4	5
Equity	6	5	4	3	2	1
Total Assets	6	6	6	6	6	6
Net Operating Assets = Invested Capital	6	6	6	6	6	6
Net Operating Income	1	1	1	1	1	1
Interest Expense	0	0.1	0.2	0.3	0.4	0.5
Net Income	1	0.9	0.8	0.7	0.6	0.5
Returnn on Net Operating Assets (= ROIC)	16.67%	16.67%	16.67%	16.67%	16.67%	16.67%
Cost of Debt (d)	10%	10%	10%	10%	10%	10%
Leverage	1	1.2	1.5	2	3	6
ROE	16.67%	18.00%	20.00%	23.33%	30.00%	50.00%

=> The higher the debt, the higher the leverage and the higher the RoE.
- Leverage only increases RoE if RNOA is greater than the cost of debt.
- $RoE = d + (RNOA - d) * leverage$
- The ratio of changes in RoE and changes in leverage reveals the excess return ratio.
- **Practical example.**
  - Business model of (traditional) banks is re-distribution of money for a fixed fee.
  - They receive money from savers and pay a little saving interest rate and give it to needers in form of a loan for a higher interest rate.

    → At all, no equity is needed; but in case of a crisis, there is no buffer against losses.

    => Therefore the growth of the leverage is limited, also because of the shrinking investment opportunities (each investment must at least generate a RNOA equal to d).

- **Quick overview.**
  - Clean surplus relation $D_t = NI_t - \Delta CE_t = Revenues - Expenses - (\Delta Assets - \Delta Liabilities)$
  - Reveals the important forecasts analysts have to make in terms of company valuation.
    - Revenue (sales growth), operating efficiency (gross margin, profit margin, etc.), changes in assets (turnover-ratios) and changes in the capital structure.

The role of accounting information in equity valuation.

- Better prediction of future cash flows are earnings rather than cash.
  - Cash doesn't take (long-term) investments into account (depreciation & amortization).
- Financial statements provide a starting point for estimations of future business activities.
- Cash from customers equals sales subtracted by receivables, but sales are more meaningful.
- Allocate the expenses to revenue where they're belonging to (matching principle).
- Accounting reveals the "true" (principle of cautiousness) situation of the company (going concern assumption) → Financial statements are a meaningful indicator of performance.

The case of doubtful receivables.

- Receivables are recognized as revenue even though they are still outstanding.
- Uncertain payment in the future, imagine the customer isn't able to pay anymore.
  - → Than the financial statements are corrected by a write-off in the next period.
- In the "long"-run the financial statements will become error-free.
  - → Effects of earnings management is only short-term.
- Accruals captures changes in non-cash assets, but include several risks.
- Write down receivables in case of not-paying customers.
- Write down inventory if it perishes
- Write down PPE if it is demolished.
  - => Creation of other expenses or losses.
- **How the financial statements are related to each other.**

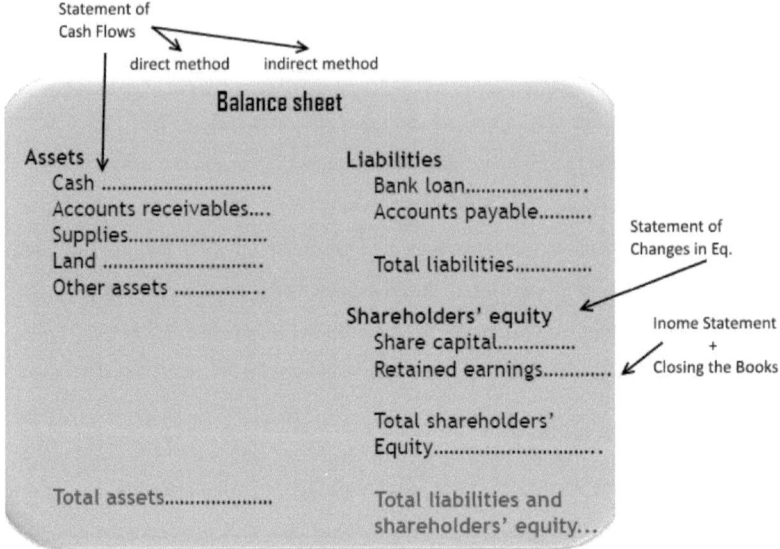

- **Derivation of financial statements (SCF out of BS and IS).**
  - (1) Compare the actual balance sheet with the one from last period and determine the changes.
  - (2) Look into the income statement to find the net income (= profit).
  - (3) Divide / adjust the profit into CFO (cash flow from operating activities), CFI (cash flow from investing activities) and CFF (cash flow from financing activities).
  - Steps to turn profit into cash (adj. Profit = adj. Sales – adj. CoGS).
  - (3.1) Adjust the sales by non-cash revenues.
  - Adjusted Sales = Sales – Δ Receivables.
  - (3.2) Adjust the CoGS by the matching principle and payables (if inventory was purchased on account).
  - Adjusted CoGS Inventory = CoGS-Inventory + Δ Inventory – Δ Payables.
  - Adjusted CoGS-CapEx = CoGS-CapEx – Depreciation (because it belongs to investing activities).
    - In NOA PPE is included, but normally it belongs to investing activities. It was only included earlier because we divided into "operating" and "financing" and not into three categories.
  - **CFO** = Profit – Δ Receivables – Δ Inventory + Δ Payables + Depreciation.
  - **CFO** = Sales – CoGS-Inventory – CoGS-CapEx – Δ Receivables – Δ Inventory + Δ Payables

+ Depreciation

- **CFI** = - (Δ Fixes Assets).

- **CFF** = Δ Other Equity (excl. R.E.) + Δ Debt – Dividends.

- **Total Δ in cash = CFO + CFI + CFF.**

- In reality many companies decide to to such an indirect cash accounting method because it is much easier than checking every single transaction whether its cash-related or not.

- Profit is more meaningful than cash, but cash is also important to reveal how long it takes to turn profit into cash.

- Profit = Δ Cash + Accruals.

- **Back to our previous example.**

  - Both companies face the same profit, but have different earnings.

  - Accruals are the intersection between cash and profit.

  - Benefit of accrual accounting: feasible performance measure (related to long-term investments); fix two timing errors (cash payments before use, performance before cash received).

> **Accruals more info than cash flow if**
> 1. long operating cycle
> 2. large growth
> 3. short interval

Summary of this chapter.

- Value of a business is determined by its expected cash flows.

- Companies invest capital in assets to generate cash flows, but cash is not costless.

- Excess return must be positive to create value (generated cashflow – WACC).

- Grow profitably is the key of company value.

- Accruals are a better performance measure rather than cash alone.

> **Exam questions**
> Use balance sheet and income statement to derive the statement of cash flows
> Use statement of cash flows to derive the balance sheet
> → **Übungsaufgaben machen!**

Profitability analysis: RoE.

- Perspective of an equity investor; equity price is reflected in the share price.

- Based on accounting numbers, which aren't always true / perfect (earnings management, conservatism).

- Minority interest and preferred stocks are treated as long-term debt holders

  - Common Equity = Equity – Minority Interest – Preferred Stocks.

- Problem: Comparing stock with flows.
- Ideally a time-weighted average of common equity would be calculated.
  → Information is not available.
- Average of the beginning and the ending is calculated ("CE bar").

Targets balance sheet		Acquirers balance sheet (before)	
Assets 50	Equity 50	Cash 40	Equity 100
		Other Assets 60	

Acquirers balance sheet (after)		Consolidated balance sheet	
Cash 0	Equity 100	Other Assets 60	Equity 100
Other Assets 60		Assets 50	Minority Interest 10
Investment 40			

$$ROE = \frac{NI_t}{\overline{CE_t}} \qquad \overline{CE_t} = \frac{CE_t + CE_{t-1}}{2}$$

Decomposing RoE – The Basic Dupont Model.

- $RoE = Net\ Profit\ Margin * Asset\ Turnover * Total\ Leverage$.

- $$RoE = \frac{Net\ Income}{Sales} * \frac{Sales}{Average\ Total\ Assets} * \frac{Average\ Total\ Assets}{Average\ Common\ Equity}.$$

$$RoE = \underbrace{\frac{NI}{Sales}}_{\text{profit margin}} * \underbrace{\frac{Sales}{Total\ Assets}}_{\text{turnover}} * \underbrace{\frac{Total\ Assets}{Equity}}_{\text{leverage}} = \frac{NI}{Equity}$$

- Basic DuPont model highlights the three key drivers of RoE.
- None of this three value drivers can be negative to reveal a positive outcome.
- **Mean-reversion** of the three key value drivers in the basic DuPont Model.
- *NPM* is very mean-revert, the lowest quintile reaches a (nearly) constant NPM after year 3, the NPM of the first quintile is constantly decreasing but still further away from the mean than the other quintiles.
- *Total asset turnover* isn't mean-revert, is very constant. The quintiles are far away from the mean and remain constant escept the first one, but only slightly decrease.
- *Leverage* is also very stable, similar to TAT. First quintile is slightly decreasing and further away from the mean than the others, they are very stable and close to the mean.
- **Conclusions**.
  - Leverage and TAT remain constant because they are determined by the business model rather than by the competition.

16

- NPM is closely related (= depended) to the competitive advantage which is influenced by competitors actions. → High margins are expected to be mean-revert; only look at NPM changes if analyzing changes in the RoE.

  => Mean-reversion of RoE is primary driven by mean-reversion of NPM.

- **Increasing the Return on Assets.**
- Company has to generate profit (npm%) a the minimum investment in asset (turnover).

  → Operations of the business must be efficient.
- Many companies face the **trade-off** of high profit margin and high turnover.

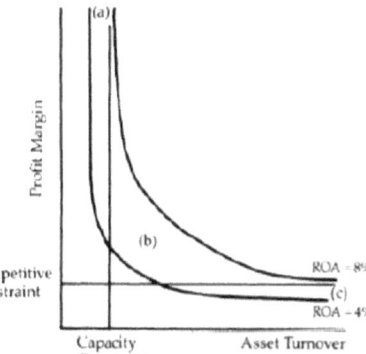

- Capital-intensive industries (construction) have low turnover and therefore must charge a higher price to increase their profit to receive a comparative RoA.
- Asset-lasting industries (discount retailers) have very high turnovers, but low margins because of the intensive competition; in the end they receive a comparative RoA by increasing their turnover-ratios.
- Isolines in the graph reveals all possible combinations of TAT and NPM to reveal the same RoA.

  - *Capacity constraint* (point (a)): Increasing inventory is restricted by high capital costs (exploration of a new oil source), therefore high margins are claimed. Only possible because this capacity constraint is a very high entry barrier.

  - *Competitive constraint* (point (c)): Companies selling (nearly) homogeneous goods face strong competition (low entry barriers) and therefore have small margins. To increase the RoA, the TAT must be increased, e.g. by minimization of fixed costs or purchase of larger quantities to realize discounts.

    => Strategy // business model determines on which side of the graph the company stays.

- **Cost leaders** selling at the lowest price possible have the smallest margins and have to ensure very high turnovers.
- **Product differentiators** must claim for high margins because their turnover is very small.

  => All companies desire both high margins and high turnovers, but in reality this is very hard to achieve.

  → The longer the wine ages, the higher the margin to sell it, but the turnover decreases.

=> If a company stays in point (b), than it is very flexible either to increase margins or to increase turnover as a reaction to changing market conditions.

- **Leveraging** the assets to increase the RoE higher than the RoA.
  - Equity investors claim for the RoA, debt investors only for the interest rate.
    → Increasing liabilities will make the slice of the cake for each equity investor bigger.
  - Companies could increase their debt ratio significantly, but this will increase risk, makes it hard to find adequate investment projects anymore and simply decreases the profit margin because of the interest expense.
- **Weaknesses** of the basic DuPont model.
- Operating and financing activities aren't separated clearly (ROA is after interest).

Accounting Analysis.

- Many forecasts and valuation models extrapolate the previous years numbers.
- **Problems** arising with this procedure.
- Non-recurring effects (sale of assets, very profitable investment) are included in accounting numbers.
- Earnings management used by managers to increase some key numbers to receive bonuses or fulfill debt covenants influences the truthfulness of the numbers.
- Accounting rules (conservatism) aren't reflecting the true situation of the company.
- **Two types of accounting distortions.**
- **(1) Aggressive accounting.**
- Overestimation of future profits, overstatement of equity or understatement of liabilities.
- Boosting profit and equity, yields an upward bias for future profits.
- Temporarily method to face important key numbers, but in the next period this will pay off by lower profits. → Downward trend because profits are borrowed from the next period.
- **(2) Conservative accounting.**
- Underestimation of future profit, overstatement of liabilities or understatement of equity.
- Better safe than sorry, used to "hide" high profits to create a buffer against losses or to beat expectations in the following periods.
  - After a takeover the new CEO can justify bad performance by restructuring activities, therefore tend to be over-cautious to beat the estimation in the next period.
- In the next period, profit is received from the last period.
- **Earnings management.**
- Accrual earnings management: aggressive or conservative accounting.

- Real earnings management: Decide to expense and not to capitalize or v.v..

  => Helps the company to generate constant returns.

- **Three sources of measurement errors.**

  - **(1) Uncertainty:** Estimations are requested and perfect estimations require perfect data and rational analysis.

	Debit		Credit	
Period 1	Cash	100	Sales	100
	Warranty Expense	40	Warranty Provision	40
Period 2	Warranty Provision	40	Inventory / Cash	50
	Loss	10		

  - Suppose the warranty provision was calculated based on previous experience, but than it turn out that more customers than "normal" claim for warranty and the accounting was wrong.

    → Understating a liability has the same effect as overstating an asset.

    → Circumstances can change in a way, the estimater hasn't taken into account.

Expensing R+D - Costs				
	Debit		Credit	
Period 1	R+D Expense	100	Cash	100
Period 2	Cash	200	Revenue	200
Capitalizing R+D - Costs				
	Debit		Credit	
Period 1	R+D Asset	100	Cash	100
Period 2	Cash	200	Revenue	200
	Amortization Exp	50	R+D Asset	50

  - **(2) Accounting methods** are often over-cautious and lead to an understatement of profits when R&D – costs are expensed (optional under IRFS, mandatory under US-GAAP).

  - **(3) Earnings management** when managers' bonuses are related to accounting numbers than they have strong incentive to use earnings management to receive these bonuses.

    => Terms "aggressive" and "conservative accounting" are misleading because sometimes it isn't a result of opportunistic behavior.

- **Profit as sum of accruals and cash.**

  - High profit can be related to high amount of accruals, but they will constantly decrease over time → profit is not sustainable.

  - Likelihood of future losses is higher than normal because accruals can not create expected economic benefit (in case of destruction etc.).

  - Companies tend to upward bias their numbers close before an IPO to generate more demand for their stocks; investors aren't fooled because all relevant information has to be disclosed in the notes of the financial statements, but nobody looks into it.

  - **Accrual Anomaly.**

    - If investors only focus on profit and not about the portion of accruals and cash flows, then they will overestimate the companies with high accruals and are disappointed in the future when the accruals as well as the earnings decrease.

EPS forecast is 5			
EPS before earnings management	4	4.9	5.5
Effect of earnings management	- 0.3	+ 0.15	- 0.45
EPS afterwards	3.7	5.05	5.05
Beat forecast?	no	yes	yes

If company is definitely not meeting the forecasts (Poor Dogs), it uses conservative accounting to beat the forecast within the next period. If a company definitely beats the forecast (Star), it will use conservative accounting to make the numbers just beat the forecast to have a buffer in the next period and not raising the expectations. Only companies close to the forecast have incentive to use aggressive accounting.

	Asset Overstatement	Liability Understatement	Asset Understatement	Liability Overstatement
Originating	Earnings Overstated		Earnings Understated	
	Failing to write down obsolete inventory	Underestimate liability from warranty claims	Failing to capitalize R&D expenditure	Excessive revenue deferral
Reversing	Earnings Understated		Earnings Overstated	
	Subsequent write down of obsolte inventory	Subsequent expenses from warranty claims not anticipated	Realization of benefits from R&D expenditure	Subsequent recognition of deferred revenue

- **Evaluate the meaningfulness of auditors' report.**
  - An objective outsider should oversee the financial statements before they are published and detect errors / fraud to protect the shareholders.
  - Shareholders can sue the auditor if they haven't detect fraud.
  - Earnings management isn't illegal, managers just use the flexibility they get from the accounting methods.
    - Disclosure requirement of all necessary information is fulfilled, but no investor cares about it.
    - Reputational concerns provoke managers not to do earnings management.
    - Using aggressive accounting all the time will lead to an downwards spiral and end in a crisis.

- **Illustrating Accounting Measurement Errors** (Slides 103 – 106).
  - **Conclusions:**
  - Cash flows aren't a good performance measure, but the economic rate of return (ERR).
    - ERR = Economic income / beginning Investment.

- Total cash flows haven't changes with earnings management, but the way these cash flows are portrayed.

Techniques of earnings management.

- **Revenue manipulation**: Send too much products and list revenue; in the next period the products return and a loss occurs.
- **Related-party transactions**: Send product to friend close before FYE and afterwards send back.
- **Off-Balance Sheet Financing**: Operating lease, no lease liability is recorded, only the rent expense.

- **Miscellaneous**.
  - **Motivation to use earnings management.**
    - Influence stock prices.
    - Pressure to meet / beat internal and external forecasts.
    - Increase the own compensation.
    - Reputation concerns (not wanted to appear as bad manager).
    - Prevent violating (negative) debt covenants.
  - **How to spot earnings management.**
    - GAAP earnings and cash flows aren't correlated to each other, earnings are increasing, but cash flows decreasing.
    - Deviations from the industry: If numbers exceeding the industry's average.
    - Consistently meet or beat the forecasts (20-25 periods in a row).
    - Having lots of accruals.
      - Compare with the industry's average balance sheet items; following assets are important.
        - **PPE**: Useful lifetime can be set very large.
        - **Intangible assets**: Stated to have indefinitely lifetime (not infinity, but can't measure).
        - **Receivables**: Underestimate / neglect the default rate.

Operating Accruals (Apple Example).

- Cash from selling products is split into a portion of the product and a portion for free updated.
  - → Only the cash portion related to the product is revenue, the rest is still outstanding.
- So called "Accrual Rate" can influence net income by earnings management.
- In periods of high income, the accrual rate can be set high and v.v..

→ Build a high warranty provision balance in stronger times to have a buffer in weak times.

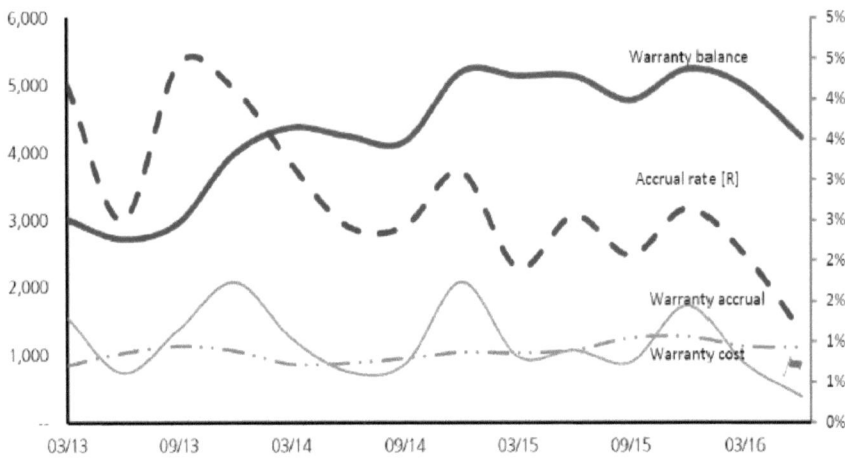

- Warranty balance of Apple at the end of 2016 was very high related to the high accrual rates from the end of 2013.
- Warranty costs are very stable, but the volatility of accrual rate provokes volatility of the warranty balance and the warranty accruals → Allows to generate constant returns.
- Now the warranty accruals are below the warranty costs, therefore the warranty balance will decrease → Net income is overstated now, because Apple must raise the accrual rate sometime. => Adjust the net income to previous quarters' accrual rates.
- **Adjustment of net income.**
  - Look into the income statement to identify the total sales and CoGS to calculate the gross margin.
  - Reduce the total sales to that portion directly belonging to the products of Apple and multiply with accrual rate from previous year to receive the adjusted warranty expense.
  - (Adjusted warranty expense minus warranty expense) must be added to the CoGS and the new, adjusted gross margin can be calculated. => Will be lower than before.
- **Reasons for decreasing deferrals rate.**
  - Could be earnings management so Apple could ensure constant returns.
  - Apple states that rate is decreased because increasing competition makes updates less valuable.
    → Boosting sales revenue when lowering the accrual rate.

=> If this change wasn't undertaken, the share price would decrease by 73 basis points.

- **Off balance sheet items – R&D – Costs.**
- Under US GAAP R&D-Costs must be expensed, under IFRS some criteria must be fulfilled that development costs can be capitalized; research costs always have to be expensed.
- Healthcare / pharmaceutical firms can't capitalize because the criteria aren't met (probable future economic benefit; because FDA can refuse the market introduction of a created drugs).
  - **Three important rations regarding R&D – Costs.**
  - R&D Investment = Capitalized development + expensed research.
  - Capitalization Ratio = Capitalized development / R&D Investment.
  - R&D Expense = Expensed Research + Amortization of all capitalized items.
- **Benchmarking across industries.**
- Companies under US GAAP (located in the US or traded at the US markets) must be eliminated because they have no choice (R&D must be expensed).
- Companies with higher capitalization rate may differ in innovative research.
  - Subsidiaries can profit from parents research (& v.v.) so less research costs.
- Total R&D Investment can be smaller than R&D costs related to amortization expenses.
- Capitalized assets can be compared with amortization costs to see if the useful lifetime is set shortly, extensively or infinitely.
- **OBS items and company valuation.**
  - **Operating expenses**: only expenses from the current period
  - **Capital expenditure**: Expenses from all periods occur in this period.
- Book value of US Tech companies is understated because most important assets are OBS.
- Deep discussion about whether to capitalize R&D costs or not.
  - Advantages: If all companies must expense their R&D costs, they can be benchmarked.
  - Disadvantages: Distortion affects different kinds of companies differently (see later).
- **Important steps to adjust for R&D costs.**
  - (1) Estimate the (average) useful lifetime of investment.
  - Some intangible assets last 10 years, others fail to generate economic benefit (0 years) and if both are weighted 50%, than 5 years is the useful lifetime.
  - (2) Estimate the amortization method.
  - (3) Determine the R&D asset.
  - (4) Adjust the profit (exclude expensed R&D investment, include amortization).
- **Numerical example for Apple.**

starting from FYE 2016, the last amortization expense affecting 2016s expense will be from 2012	R&D m$		In 2016 Amortized		Amortized	At end of 2016 Remaining capitalized	
2012	3,381	20%	20%	676.20	100%	0%	0.00
2013	4,475		20%	895.00	80%	20%	895.00
2014	6,041		20%	1,208.20	60%	40%	2,416.40
2015	8,067		20%	1,613.40	40%	60%	4,840.20
2016	10,045		20%	2,009.00	20%	80%	8,036.00

annual R&D investments of Apple

Amortization **6,401.80**

Amortization expense for 2016

R&D Asset **16,187.60**
How much of the asset is still on the balance sheet at FYE 2016

- Adjust Assets by: + 16,187.5
- Adjust Profit by: + 3,643.2 (10,045 − 6,401.8)
- Adjust Retained Earnings by: + 12,544.3 (16,187.5 − 3,643.2)

- Reported Profit: 45,687
- Adjusted Profit: 49,330.2
- Reported Equity: 128,249
- Adjusted Equity: 144,436.5 (+3,643.2 & + 12,544.3)

- Reported ROE: 35.62% (uses ending equity only)
- Adjusted ROE: 34.15% (uses ending equity only)

- **Adjustment of net income in the Apple example.**
  - Operating expenses → R&D costs will be changed to amortization expense.
  - Operating income will be adjusted by difference of recorded and adjusted R&D costs.

Performance comparison of start-ups and older companies.

- Capitalizing the R&D costs will first increase the profits and ROE, but when the useful lifetime of the first recorded asset is reached, than the ROE and profits will be lower than with expensing.
- All US firms have to expense their R&D costs therefore some people argue this makes US firms comparable with each other.
- BUT: Start-ups can't be compared with older firms because they aren't existing for long and wrong data would be extrapolated.
- Capitalizing R&D costs will increase both ROE and profits of a start-up.
  => Only with capitalized R&D costs old and young companies can be compared.

- **Insights from Capitalizing R&D Costs.**
- Companies performance is measured more reliably, but its value hasn't changed because no cash flows are changed, only the perception was adjusted.
  → Return on Equity will be lowered, but also the growth is increased, therefore Residual Income Method reveals the same valuation (both effects cancel each other out).
- **Main reasons for undertaking this adjustment.**

- (1) Present the investment more accurately, matching principle, prevent the understatement of the investment.
- (2) Prevent manipulation of short term earnings, created incentive to cut down R&D costs to meet earnings target, meet targets to the harm of the future.
- (3) Improve performance assessment, expensing masks result of dropped performance because R&D budget is percentage related to revenue.

Criteria for Capitalization.

- Advertisement costs are wanted to be capitalized too because they increase the brand equity and therefore provide future economic benefit.
  → Same line of argumentation for recruitment costs.
- There must be substantial evidence of future economic benefit occurring over multiple periods of time.
- We're trying to estimate the value of investment, not the market value of R&D or brand asset, only about allocating the expenses to the future benefits.
  => Therefore, to be consistent, R&D costs can't be capitalized in the US, "better save than sorry", conservative accounting.

- **Off Balance Sheet Financing (OBS-financing).**
  - Operating lease will create no lease asset and no related lease liability, only a rent expense.
    → Total Asset Turnover, Debt Ratio and Leverage are distorted.
  - Reasons to do so are the attraction of more investors, but also increased flexibility.
    - Leasing stores instead of owning them will make the company better off. If the store becomes unattractive, the company must sell it; but because it is unattractive nobody wants to buy it (or only with huge losses). Lease companies must buy them back if lease contract was canceled (and receive some fee, but less than the loss in the other case).
  - **Adjustment for Operating Lease** (capitalize it).
    - Rent consists of two components $Rent = Depreciation + Interest\ Expense$.
    - $$Asset\ Value_{t-1} = \frac{Rent_t}{\frac{1}{Asset\ Life} + interest\ rate}$$.
  - The interest rate is related to the cost of debt; use the actual debt cost (if the company has any debt, otherwise assume an adequate interest rate).
  - In the annex of the financial statements, there is a depreciation for the related lease assets.

- Using the data from the balance sheet and income statement to calculate the value of the lease assets (*for the last period*).
- To calculate the asset value for the *actual period* estimate the rent for this period.
- $Rent_t = \dfrac{Rent_{t-1}}{Stores_{t-1}} * Stores_t$ And then use the formula above to calculate the asset value.

- **Adjust the related numbers in the balance sheet and the income statement.**
  - Add the lease asset to the total assets for this period and the last period and calculate the average total assets too.
  - Common Equity and Net Income won't be changed, only Leverage and Total Asset Turnover.
    → Asset Turnover will decrease, Leverage will increase.
    => Even though the numbers change, the ROE doesn't change since the effects perfectly cancel each other out.
  - In case of insolvency, the lease payments have to be paid with Retained Earnings / Equity (negative ROA) → Higher leverage will make everything worse.
    => Higher leverage = higher risk → Reveals the true default risk of the firm.

- **Split up the rent into depreciation and interest.**

$Rent_t = Depreciation_t + Interest\ Expense_t \qquad Rent_t = \dfrac{Asset\ Value_{t-1}}{Asset\ Life} + Asset\ Value_{t-1} \times d$

$20{,}554 = \dfrac{137{,}026.\overline{67}}{8.33} + 137{,}026.\overline{67} \times 0.03 = 16{,}443.2\ (Depreciation) + 4{,}110.8\ (Interest\ Expense)$

- Interest expense will increase the operating profit (=EBIT), but not the net income because the total interest expense will be increased and subtracts the operating profit.

- **Conclusions from the lease adjustments.**
  - When the company takes a loan to buy an asset, both are recorded in the balance sheet and interest expenses will lower net income (loan installments don't).
  - When company uses operating lease, the lessee will only face a rent expense.
  - Artificial high capital productivity (TAT) and low operating profits because of the smaller amount of assets → Both effects cancel each other out and don't influence the ROE.
  - Wall Street formula to calculate the lease liability (= lease asset): 8 * Rent Expense.
    → Not very precise, but better than no adjustment; 8 is derived from (1 over asset life + d)$^{-1}$.

- **Significant Events and their Accounting Implications.**

- If some great disaster happens, the company must create provisions (in addition to the costs of the direct response).
- Provisions of the oil disaster of BP are 50% lower than the market estimations.
  - Total provision is the sum of all expenses that are "more likely than not" to occur in the future and BP estimated to win most of the law suits because they argued it wasn't their fault.
    → In the end the amount of provisions was increased over the last 6 years and now its very close to the previous market estimation.
- Contingent liabilities arose and are only recognized in the annex of the financial statements.
- Provisions only decrease the retained earnings (debt swap), doesn't mean to set cash aside.
- GAAP often require companies to recognize provisions if future losses are likely to occur.
  → If criteria for a provision aren't met, only a contingent liability is disclosed.

- **Non-recurring events.**
- There are some expenses that are non-recurring or pro-forma earnings (not regulated in the GAAP).
- Company will try to classify as much expenses as possible to be non-recurring to increase the key numbers of operating performance.
  → Earnings management: overestimate the nonrecurring expenses (conservative accounting).
- Typical non-recurring costs are: impairments, foreign currency exchanges losses / gains, gains / losses on legal settlements.
  - Restructuring charges. Occurs when the CEO of a company changes, incentive to do conservative accounting and estimate the non-recurring expenses to be very high to increase important key numbers over the next periods.

Red flags to identify misuse of non-recurring expenses.

- Income from unspecified sources, from asset sales.
- Sudden changes in standard expense items (changes in ratio of R&D costs and revenue, because R&D budget is related to total revenue).
- Frequent accounting restatements (if someone finds out that there is a accounting mistake / fraud).
- Accrual earnings are significantly higher than cash flows.
- Differences between tax income and reported income.

- **Entity vs. Equity Perspective.**

- $ROE = \dfrac{NI.}{CE}$ Includes financing activities, so not very useful.

- $'ROA' = \dfrac{NI.}{TA}$ Includes financing activities and gross operating liabilities.

- $ROA = \dfrac{EBIT}{TA}$ Before tax, but includes financial assets.

- $ROA = \dfrac{NOI}{TA}$ Financial assets still included, but interest revenue eliminated from numerator.

- $RNOA = \dfrac{NOI}{NOA}$ Best measure of operating performance.

  $\rightarrow$ Nets Operating Liabilities with Operating Assets and Debt with Financial Assets.

- **Advanced DuPont Model.**
- Basic DuPont Model mixes up financing and operating activities.
- Separate operating (entity pov) from financing activities (equity / debt pov).

  - $ROE = RNOA + Leverage * Spread = \dfrac{NOI}{NOA} + \dfrac{NFO}{CE} * \left(RNOA - NBC\right)$
- **Transform the balance sheet.**
  - Operating Assets are subtracted by operating liabilities to reveal the NOA.
    $\rightarrow$ Eliminate financial assets from the asset side.
  - Financial liabilities are subtracted by financial assets to reveal the net financial obligation
    NFO $\rightarrow$ NFO + Equity = IC = NOA.
- **Transform the income statement.**
  - Normally the interim results are: Gross Profit, EBIT, EBT and Net Income.
  - Turn them into the following.
  - Gross Profit remains unchanged.
  - EBIT is just renamed to NOI (b4 tax).
  - From the NOI (b4 tax) the tax expense is subtracted to reveal the NOI (after tax).
  - Interest income and interest expense turn the NOI (after tax) into the NFE (b4 tax).
  - Tax shield (NFE * interest rate) is added to the NFE (b4 tax) to reveal the NFE (after tax).
  - NOI (after tax) + NFE (after tax) = Net Income.
- **Operating Activities =** $RNOA = NOM * NOAT = \dfrac{NOI}{Sales} * \dfrac{Sales}{NOA} = \dfrac{NOI}{NOA}$

  - RNOA equals Net Operating Margin times Net Operating Asset Turnover.
- **Financing Activities =** $Net\ Borrowing\ Costs\left(NBC\right) = \dfrac{NFE}{NFO}$

- Net Borrowing Costs equal Net Financing Expense over Net Financial Obligation (balance sheet).
- **Gain / Loss from financing activities.**
  - $Leverage * Spread = \dfrac{NFO}{CE} * \left(RNOA - NBC\right)$

  => RNOA + Gain/Loss from financing activities = Return on Equity.
  - $ROE = RNOA + Leverage * Spread = \dfrac{NOI}{NOA} + \dfrac{NFO}{CE} * \left(RNOA - NBC\right)$.
- **The Advanced DuPont (extended).**
  - $ROE = NOM * NOAT + Leverage * Spread = \dfrac{NOI}{Sales} * \dfrac{Sales}{NOA} + \dfrac{NFO}{CE} * \left(\dfrac{NOI}{NOA} - \dfrac{NFE}{NFO}\right)$.

  → NOM * NOAT + Leverage * Spread.

- **Miscellaneous**.
- Many companies hold cash and cash equivalents (financial assets (shares) which can be turned into cash very quickly (on daily basis)).
- Cash includes an operating and a financing component.
  → Rule of thumb: historical average 5% of sales = operating cash
- Total cash & cash equivalents – operating cash = excess cash (→ financing activities).
  - **Reasons for having so many cash.**
    - Protection against hostile takeovers, but enables to do takeovers quickly.
    - Increasing flexibility against banking crisis (when banks won't borrow cash anymore).
    - **Tax prevention**: Shifting capital to other countries (Ireland) will reduce the total tax expense, but when moving to the US, than the total amount of tax has to be paid.
- **Leverage**: Return to debt is not related to operating performance; if borrowing cash for a lower interest rate than the investment generates, than this will increase the (cash) profits and the total amount of capital which can be distributed to equity holders.
  - Equity holder gain from debt holders because upside payments to debt holders are limited by the interest rate; equity holders have no upside limit (operating return).
- If ROE is driven by financing activities, suppose the operating activities goes negative, than the whole leverage effect will turn the performance negative.

- **Calculate the reasons for the negative financing effect.**
  - *Financing Effect = Leverage * Spread*

- Negative net financial obligation because having more financial assets than debt.
- **Transform the income statement and the balance sheet.**
- Calculate the financial assets by total cash & cash equivalents subtracted by the operating cash (5% of revenues).
  - *Financial Assets = Cash & Cash Equivalents – Operating Cash.*
- Operating assets are then total assets subtracted by financial cash.
  - *Operating Assets = Total Assets – Financial Cash*
- Debt equals long-term and short-term debt in the balance sheet and will be subtracted from the total liabilities to reveal the operating liabilities.
  - *Operating Liabilities = Total Liabilities – Total Debt*
- Applying the advanced DuPont model, than the net financial assets (*Debt – Financial Assets = NFA*).

Microsoft Balance Sheet converted 2015

Net Operating Assets	23,528	Equity	80,083
		Net Financial Obligations	-56,555

Net Operating Assets	23,528	Equity	80,083
Net Financial Assets	56,555		

→ Negative liabilities are a financial asset (economic perspective).

- Alternative we could leave the netting process out and left the gross financial obligation (Debt + Financial Assets = Business Assets).

Microsoft Balance Sheet convertedx3 2015

Business Assets	Net Operating Assets	23,528	Equity	80,083
	Financial Assets	91,847	Debt	35,292

→ No real word, only used to make procedure easier.

- **Calculate the NOI and the NFI (net financial income).**
- Net operating income = reported EBIT minus the operating portion of the other expenses and after taxation.
- *Net financial income* = Interest revenue subtracted by interest expense and after taxation.

  → If only „other income" is listed in the income statement, then look into the annex of the financial statements to find those numbers.

Income Statement 2015 converted	
Reported Operating Income	18,161
Other Operating Income (Loss)	-355
Operating Income	17,806
Net Operating Income	**11,731.16**
Financial Income (Expense)	701
Net Financial Income (Expense)	**461.84**

30

- The *efficient tax rate* = tax payment over EBT

=> Net financial income occurs if the interest expense is smaller than the interest revenue.

- **Calculating the single components of the advanced DuPont model.**

· RNOA 49.86%	· Leverage -0.71	· Spread 49.04%	· ROE = 15.23%

- Leverage effect is negative.

=> In 95% of all cases the leverage will be positive, if not, than search for the reason.

=> Whenever one component is negative, find out why.

- **Explain why the ROE of Microsoft is so low.**
  - **First alternative: Using the advanced DuPont model.**
    - Having calculated the NOA and the NFA enables to identify the portion of IC which each of both asset classes belongs to.

RNOA = NOI / NOA	49.86%
RNFA = NFI / NFA	0.82%
ROE = RNOA x NOA/Equity + RNFA x NFA/Equity	15.23%
ROE = NI / Equity	15.23%

  - Calculating the RNOA and the RNFA reveals that the operating assets generate a return of nearly 50% whereas the financial assets not even generate 1%.

    => Difference between the RNOA and the ROE is determined by more than 70% of the total assets are NFA which generate less than 1% return.

- $$ROE = RNOA * \frac{NOA}{Equity} + RFNA * \frac{NFA}{Equity}$$

  - **Second alternative: Using a more intuitive approach.**
    - Leaving the financial assets un-netted and grouping them to „Business Assets" (NOA + FA).

RNOA = NOI / NOA	49.80%
RFA = FI / FA	1.06%
ROBA = (NOI+FI) / (NOA+FA)	11.01%
BC = FE / Debt	1.46%
Leverage** = Debt/ Equity	0.44
Spread = ROBA - BC	9.56%
ROE = ROBA + Leverage** × Spread	15.23%

  - By calculating the numbers, the same result is revealed.

Important Valuation Ratios.

- **Margin ratios (GM, NOM)**: Comparison between profit/loss and other items from the income statement.
- **Turnover ratios (NOAT, TAT)**: Compare sales to a balance sheet item.
- **Return / profitability ratios (ROE)**: Compare some item from the income statement with some item from the right side of the balance sheet.
- **Capital structure ratios**: Compare items from equity with such from debt.

- **Asset structure ratios**: Compare items from the right side of the balance sheet with each other.
- **Liquidity ratios**: Compare Assets with items form the right side of the balance sheet.
=> Compare flows (sum over the period) only with averages of stocks (average common equity).

- **Turnover Ratios.**
  - **Working capital** is the capital available for the daily business (*current operating assets minus current operating liabilities*).
  - Calculate several ratios to reveal how often during one financial year the average amount was replaced by new items or how long the average asset / liability stays within the company.

$$Receivables\ Turn_t = \frac{Sales_t}{Trade\ Receivables_t} \qquad Days\ to\ Collect\ Receivables_t = \frac{365}{Receivables\ Turn_t}$$

$$Inventory\ Turn_t = \frac{COGS_t}{Inventory_t} \qquad Inventory\ Holding\ Period_t = \frac{365}{Inventory\ Turn_t}$$

$$Payables\ Turn = \frac{Purchases_t}{Trade\ Payables_t} = \frac{\Delta Inventory_t + COGS_t}{Trade\ Payables_t} \qquad Days\ to\ Pay\ Payables_t = \frac{365}{Payables\ Turn_t}$$

- **Operating cycle** describes the time between buying the asset until receiving cash for selling it.
- **Cash conversion cycle** describes the time between paying for the asset and receiving the cash.
=> Both cycles are wanted to be decreased, sometimes companies realize even negative CCC's.
- A negative CCC reveals that the company is very efficient in the usage of their assets.

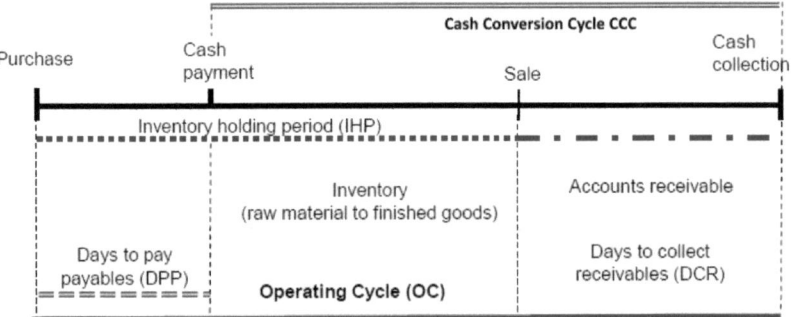

- **What does a high Inventory Holding Period (IHP) reveals?**
  - *Apple* has a <u>low</u> IHP because it outsourced all its manufacturing tasks and „buys" their product from the contract partner and sells them directly to the clients. Furthermore the clients wait for the products and directly buy them.
  - *Phillip Morris* has a <u>high</u> IHP because their products (tobacco) has to age.

- **Credit risk of firms.**
  - Having a high *leverage* means that when the spread turns out to be negative, the whole downward effect is boosted by the leverage.
  - *Debt to equity ratio* is also one very reliable measure of risk even though being very simple.
  - *Cash flow from operating activities or funds from operating activities* are divided by debt to reveal investors how profitable the company is.
  - In case of bankruptcy the debt holders receive a stack of the operating assets and therefore want to know how profitable these assets are.
  - *Funds from operations*: Net income + Depreciation + Amortization.

- **Short-term liquidity.**
  - *Current ratio*: Should always be larger than one, indicated that the company has some working capital (more current assets than current liabilities).
  - *Quick ratio*: Reduce the current assets to cash & cash equivalents and receivables (factoring) because they can be turned immediately into cash.
  - *Interest coverage ratios* are also important, compare the EBIT(DA) with the total amount of interest payments to reveal

$$C(F)FO\ to\ Debt = \frac{C(F)FO_t}{Debt_t}$$

$$Current\ ratio_t = \frac{Current\ Assets_t}{Current\ Liabilities_t}$$

$$Quick\ ratio = \frac{Cash\ and\ Equivalents_t + Receivables_t}{Current\ Liabilities_t}$$

$$EBIT(DA)\ Interest\ Coverage_t = \frac{EBIT(DA)_t}{Interest\ Expense_t}$$

  whether a company is likely to fulfill their financial obligation.
    - Many negative debt covenants require this ratio to be higher than 6.
  - **Comparing this ratios with each other** to reveal some basic insights into the company.
    - If EBIT interest coverage ratio is much smaller than EBITDA interest coverage ratio means that the company is very asset-heavy.
    - If the current ratio is close to the quick ratio, this indicated that the company has lots of cash & cash equivalents in its balance sheet.

Sustainable growth rate.

  - SGR = ROE * (1 – dividend payout ratio).
  - Growth expectation without any additional external financing (minimum growth; could be enhanced with external finance)
  - Measure of internal finance available (indicated increase or decrease of Retained Earnings).
  - If company predicts a growth larger than the SGR, than they must convince the public how.

- Increase the ROE (become more profitable).
- Raise external finance (pay attention to the excess return and risk).
- Cut dividends → Investors dislike this, no option.
  → If company pays put no dividends, than SGR equals ROE.

- **Structured Forecasts**.
  - Go back to the basic value driver of the company.
  - Goal is to question the predicted (mis-)success of a company or the followed goals.
  - Ratios are the natural laws of one company, reflected in the past numbers.
  - Most important is the **forecast of sales** because in the end, everything depends on sales.
    - *Forecast the future interest expense*: Depends on future amount of debt, which is influenced by the profitability of operating assets what is expressed in future sales.

- **How to structure your forecast**.
  - Start from the right side; when forecasted the sales and the asset turnover, the NOA can be derived.

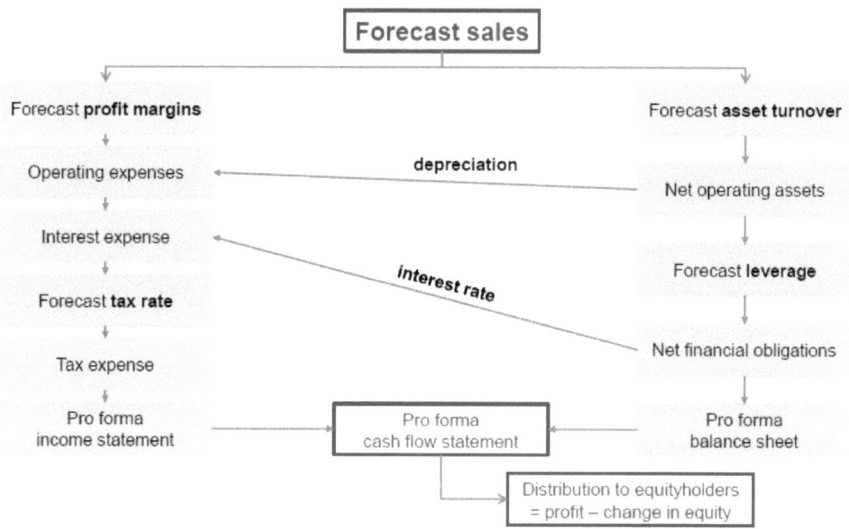

=> Never forecast the cash flows, only derive them from the key value drivers.

- **Numerical Example.**
  - Sales = 100, gross margin = 15%, NOAT = 2, useful lifetime of NOAT = 10 years, leverage =

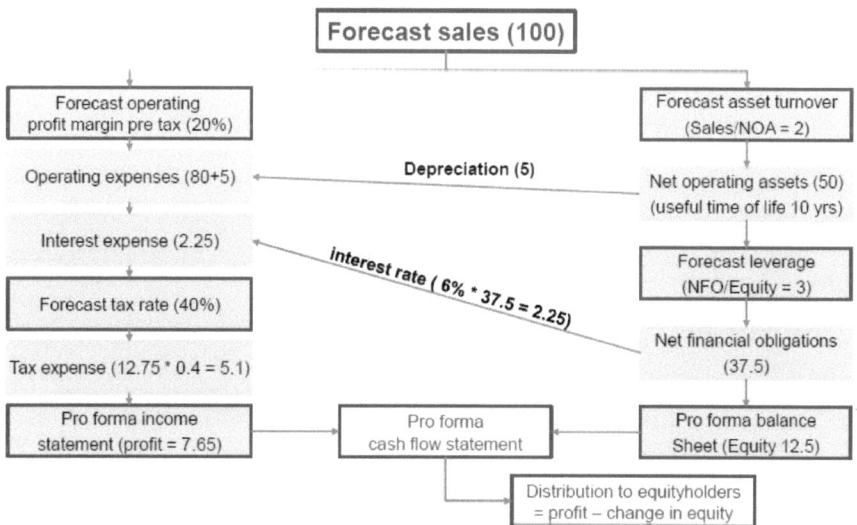

3, interest rate on debt = 6% and effective tax rate = 40%.

- When forecasted this numbers, the pro-forma financial statements can be calculated.

- NOA = Equity + NFO = 50   NFO / Equity = 3
- NFO = 3 * Equity   50 = 4 * Equity $\rightarrow$ Equity = 12, 5   NFO = 37,5

- **Forecasting horizon.**
  - Forecast the (sales) growth and ROE, but not only for the next year but also for a longer period.
  - *Short-term forecasts*: very detailed, financial statements can be forecasted relatively well.
  - *Intermediate-term forecast*: analyse industry growth and market trends, calculate how fast the company converges to the average; don't overestimate the competitive advantage.
  - *Terminal year*: The point in time at which the forecasted numbers for the last year equal the numbers for this and the following year. ROE converges close to the WACC; growth to the long-term average (average annual GDP growth: 2%).

- **Value drivers of sales growth.**
  - **Three channels for sales growth**: industry sale growth, size of the market share, entering / enter of new new industries.
  - **Three drivers of sales growth**: increase capacity, increase turnover, increase the price of the product.
  - But the sales growth isn't always linear depending on other financial statements items.
    - **CoGS** will increase less with increasing sales because of economies of scale.
    - **SGA** are fixed costs and can't be decreased when sales fall.
    - **Inventory** may become obsolete or damaged.